Anchoring Me

Nicole Hartley

"Maybe we will meet again,
many years from now,
and our souls will remember
the fire that was started
when we were younger."

Foreword

I spent my life believing that love conquers all, that love must win, that there must be a happily ever after if it's powerful enough. But after us, I learned that some loves are bigger than just one lifetime. Some loves have existed for so much longer than this moment. Some loves are meant to guide you before they leave you to find your own destiny with the faith that you will meet again after this life is over. So to you, thank you for guiding me and for loving me.

I realized tonight
how much my life
has changed
since you left.
All good things.
It hurts so much
that I can't share them
with you.
I would have
rambled and laughed
before I got to
the funny parts.
You loved when I did that.
Now I am just
going through the motions
in a life I wish I could
enjoy with you.

All these letters,
I wanted them to
lead you back to me.
Crazy, right?
So instead,
I wrote them
for the closure
I still need.
Maybe you'll never
read a single word.
And maybe you
don't miss me
the way I miss you.
Maybe it was all
in my head.
Maybe I was
not worth loving.
Not the way
I loved you.

When we met,
I wanted to protect you.
I could feel the pain
that was obviously
buried deep inside you.
I wanted to make you smile.
Instead,
I became a source
of more pain for you.
And I'm sorry.

I don't use the headphones
I bought when we would
talk all day as we worked.
They don't fit as well
without your voice
coming through them.
And now,
my days are quiet
without you.

Remember that night
we laughed for three hours?
When I told you
about the angel
that fell in love
and gave up his wings
in the story with the song
that became ours?
I tried to convince you
that it happened recently
but it made you laugh harder
when you found out
it was twenty years old.
My face hurt
from smiling so much.
I told you that
I loved hearing you laugh.
What I wanted to say was,
that was the first time
I truly saw you
with me forever.
That was weeks ago
and now,
I can't remember

why I even told you
that story.
In a few more months,
I will have forgotten
the way your laugh
sounded too.

I started smoking weed
after you left.
The silence got
too heavy to bear.
I spent many hours
of the night,
surrounded by quiet walls.
But the drugs help,
the world stops existing
and sometimes,
I even hear you laughing
in my ear.
If I concentrate more,
I can even feel
your   hands on me.
I worry that I
may get addicted.
But if I stop,
I won't hear you
ever again.

I haven't imagined
how comforting
a cold gun would feel
on my temple
in months.
Now,
I'm constantly wishing
that I had met you
after I saved myself.

I had nothing
to offer you.
I already built a full life
in a world I could never
bring you into.
After you left,
I checked out.
I couldn't live
in this place
that took you
away from me.
I needed to
leave it behind
before I lost myself
completely.
The ground at the bottom
was cold and hard,
especially without you.
I wouldn't let myself
feel anything except
this boiling hot anger
that kept me warm.
I built a new life.
I found new people

that were worthy of my time.
I finally followed my dream,
what else did I have to lose?
I have a life I'm proud of now.
A life worthy of
a partner to share it with.
I knew who I was
a very long time ago.
The life I have built now
finally allows me
to accept that person.

My feet stood frozen in place
as I watched her button up
her shirt today,
from the bottom
to the top.
I couldn't help myself,
I asked why.
And her innocent reply was,
"If I start at the bottom,
I won't make a mistake."
My heart broke again that day,
as I stood face to face
with my little girl
that reminded me
so much of you.
As if you taught her that,
as if she was ours
in another world.
And maybe she was,
in another life.
Maybe you let me
keep her in this one
because you knew
I would need

a part of you to survive.
Or maybe,
I am crazier than I think
to believe something
so absurd.

Your couch...
Just the word
sends shivers
down my spine
straight into a
pulsing between
my thighs.

Do you ever
stop yourself
from calling me?
When you have
a bad day,
do you wonder
how I would fix it?
And when you're happy,
do you wish I were
celebrating with you?
Because I'm still here,
wishing it never ended.

You made me greedy.
I know how much
you gave me,
but I still wanted more.
I wanted everything,
I couldn't help myself.
I would get jealous
over an ex you had
long forgotten.
And I hated sharing
you with anyone else.
You completely
consumed me.
I wanted all of you.
The past,
present,
and future.

Do you remember the
day you got really sick?
It wouldn't go away.
My mind imagined
the worst.
It was the first time
in my life that I felt
the fear of losing someone.
I had never believed
that I was capable
of that much care
for someone.
I thought I was too selfish.
But that moment changed
how I looked at myself too.
I had spent so many years
with other people
until I found you.
And I could no longer
envision a future
in which you did not exist.

I woke up to
147 messages today.
None of them
were from you.

You told me once
that if I ever
pushed you away,
you would convince yourself
that I would be happier
without you.
I pushed you away.
You let me go.
And guess what?
I'm not happier.

I met someone else.
A month after you.
Another engineer with
incredible blue eyes.
Someone supportive
who let me talk for hours.
I let them into
the darkest parts
of me and they did not run.
But those beautiful eyes
were not yours.
That laugh,
was so different from yours.
And I was so very much
still yours.

I just need you to know:
I was happiest when
I was making you happy.
I was happy when you
told me what you needed,
I loved being able to deliver.
I was happy when I
drove you crazy
and caused you to
do things you never
thought you would.
I was happy when
you let me in
because I earned your trust.
I loved being able
to comfort you.
I miss making you happy.

During the last fight,
you said it felt as if
you reminded me
of everything
I wanted to run from.
I said you were
and I was an idiot.
I don't want to run from you,
you are everything
I want to run to.

I heard that people
who lose a limb
eventually learn
to live without it.
They survive,
they excel,
and they heal.
They can still
be happy even if
they are not whole.
That is the way
in which I miss you.
I survived,
I healed,
I excelled,
and I'm happier
than I've ever been.
But still,
every night,
I ache for the
part of me that
I'll never get back.

Remember that night
we agreed to stay up
and talk for hours?
However, by 1am,
you heard me
start to slur
because I was
already half asleep.
You began telling me stories
and I eventually fell asleep
to the sound of your voice.
When I woke up,
you were still on the phone,
quietly watching TV.
I would have fought it much
harder if I had realized
I was tired.
I asked why you didn't
just tell me to sleep,
and you said because
you knew me too well.
Therefore,
you decided to stay
until my exhaustion

took over.
And all I want,
is to fall asleep
to your voice.
One more time.

The commitment became
real for me the day
you gave me
your Netflix login.
Maybe it was stupid
and maybe it didn't
really matter much.
Maybe it was the
domestic aspect of it.
All I know is,
I saw a future
where we shared
so much more.

As I started to move on
and date new people,
I realized an important truth.
You were as broken as I was.
No, not in the same way.
Not as obvious.
But deep down,
you were broken.
I couldn't see it then
and I don't believe
you even knew.
Now as I heal,
I can see it.
The insecurities that haunt you.
The weight of expectation
on your shoulder.
I see it now.
I am still certain
that we could be
incredible together.
And maybe,
this time around,
I would heal you.

I got a new car.
An Audi.
I drove to Jersey and
the ride was so smooth,
I didn't even notice
I was going 80 MPH.
I thought of you
every single second
for an hour and a half.
How could I not?
You willingly traded
an Audi for a Ford.
The longer I drove,
the more I wanted to crash
this "perfect" Audi
and drive your fucking Ford.

I don't build myself
a cocoon out of my
blankets anymore.
It never feels right.
I'm either too hot
or too cold.
And I can't figure out
why I'm so uncomfortable
in my own bed.

I have been drawn to you
since the day we met.
Remember,
when you told me
about your ex?
I wanted to protect you
even though you were
a stranger.
There was a magnetic pull
that I could never understand.
And from day one,
I have been fighting
with everything
inside of me
to protect you.
But I lost,
and I hurt you.
I am sorry
that I was so
hard to love.

We were together
for such a short time
but you consumed
my heart and
I could not remember
what life was like
before you.
After you were gone,
I was surrounded
by everyone I knew,
while my mind
and my heart
were still running
back to you.

Do you remember
the way I would tell stories?
I drifted off into
several directions
but you made sure
to ask questions
until I finished each story.
And that was everything
we ever were.
I was the arrow,
and you were my anchor.

Even though
I refused to say
the words,
please know that
I have been yours
since the day
I said hello.
And I'm sorry
that I ever
made you doubt it.

I am sorry that
I didn't know
how to deal
with your insecurity.
I didn't understand it.
What did you have
to be insecure about?
You were brilliant,
kind, loving, patient,
sexy, and funny.
I couldn't understand
what you thought
you were missing.
Yes, this world makes it hard
to believe you are sexy.
But how could you
doubt it when I wanted you
as badly as I did?
I felt sexy because
you wanted me.
Why didn't you trust me too?
I'm so angry at you
for letting your insecurity win.
I know I didn't make it easy,

but I wanted you so much.
I tried to fight my demons,
I really did.
All I needed was
reassurance from you.
I trusted you.
I believed in you.
I needed you.
But sometimes,
it felt like you fed me
to the wolves.

Anchoring Me

I don't miss you
all the time.
I don't even
think of you
every day.
There are days
I'm busy
and days I'm angry
you aren't here.
Sometimes,
I lock you out of my mind
and throw away the key.
I refuse to let you in,
especially when I'm happy
and the memory of you
is banging at the door.
Yet, no matter how hard I try,
a part of me is
always missing you.

You were an addiction
I didn't want to recover from
and a fire I wanted to
burn in forever.

Remember all those
mornings you would
wake up at 5am for me?
Your voice was low
and sleepy
and God,
how it turned me on.
You would know,
from the way
I said your name
just what kind of mood
I was in.
Those were the moments
I fell in love with you.
And those moments
between waking up and
falling back to sleep,
those are the moments
I am still yours.

I am angry,
and I am so lost
in a place that
I don't want to be in.
I am tired,
and my energy is gone.
This world is breaking me.
And all I can think is,
are you still
proud of me now?

I don't know
how to move on.
Not when we promised
each other so many things.
Not when I am still
waiting,
and praying,
for you to come back.
And I realize now,
that the fear of
leaving you behind
has completely
crippled me.

I don't know if
you ever loved me
and I certainly don't know
if you still want me.
I'm not sure if you miss me
or if you ever
think of trying again.
I can't help but wonder
if you are happier without me.
But if you are choosing to stay
away even though you want me,
then you're a chicken.

Yeah, I said it.
Chicken.
Bawk.

And I cannot change you.
You have never been
an outgoing risk taker.
And I,
I have always been
on the verge of
pure oblivion.

I never told you,
but you have always
been worth the fight.
No matter how much
my demons tortured me,
please know
that I would have
happily fought them
every single day
as long as you
were by my side.

I saw a wolf dog today.
It was charcoal
with beautiful blue eyes.
I hated dogs before we met.
You on the other hand,
loved them so much
and you were
amazing with them.
I loved making you happy
so I agreed to check
some out with you.
As long as you promised
to walk it in the mornings
and train it.
You got so excited
and told me I could
even name him Hades.
I have to confess
something to you.
I started imagining
what that commitment
would be like.
I looked forward to it.
I even imagined

taking it for walks,
at night of course.
Now I find myself
mourning a dog and a life
I never thought I wanted.

My business partner
has your last name.
And my new friend
has your first name.
I couldn't use it
the first few days we met.
Last week I played a game,
both my opponents
had your name.
Today, I found a new artist
with both your middle
and last name.
You surround me
but you,
are no longer here.

I still play the lottery.
I want to buy us a house
like I promised I would.
With a yard for Hades
and a big screen television
for you to watch soccer.
We can build a state of the art
bathroom with a huge tub
to spend hours in.
If I do,
will you come home?

Sex was always
weird for me.
As much as I wanted it,
I would still feel dirty after.
I hated looking at myself
in the mirror.
Until you.
You made me feel beautiful
and feel beyond sexy.
I loved how seeing me
would make you stutter.
You respected me so much.
To the point that it
annoyed me sometimes.
All I wanted was for you
to tell me you need me now.
But you would never
put yourself before me.
I know now it was stupid.
I used it against you.
I let my demons convince me
that you didn't want me.
At times, I even let them
convince me that sex

was all you wanted.
I let them hurt us both
because I have never
craved anyone
the way I craved you.
I ruined it.
I ruined us.

After one of my lows,
you wondered if you
were the issue.
That my demons
must be attacking
because you are a bad person.
I cannot remember
what my answer was,
but I have one now.
You scared my demons.
They targeted you
because no one else
ever came close
to getting rid of them
for good.
I suppose they won.
You're gone now
and they have me
all to themselves again.

My God,
if only you knew
how often I want
to reach out to you
only to remind myself
that you are not mine.

I never told you this,
but you restored
my faith in humanity.
I lost it a long time ago,
when I realized the
world broke me.
I hated society
and everything human.
I turned off my emotions
and detached myself
from this cold life.
Then you came along
and showed me a kindness
I had never thought possible.
I remember your grandmother
called once and told you
she locked herself
out of her house.
I asked if you needed
to go deal with it.
But after the first time
she did that,
you bought a locked box
and drilled it in

the back of the house.
You hid the key in there
for the next time
it would happen.
I responded with,
"That's sexy as fuck"
and I meant it.
In that moment,
my faith in humanity
 was restored.
Because if there wasn't
any goodness and
you were the only
fucking good in
this whole world,
then my mission
would be to make this
a planet deserving of you.

The day my mother
told me she wished
I were dead,
I tried to stay strong.
I put up my walls so high
and pretended everything
was fine.
It never happened.
You, on the other hand,
refused to accept that.
I had never seen you that upset.
I think it may have
hurt you more than
it hurt me.
You never did forgive her for that.
And I guess neither have I.
I always felt so safe with you.

Do you still think
about me in
your soccer jersey?
Do you still think
of the day I wore it for you?
God, it still turns me on
when I remember
your reaction.
By the way,
you owe me a soccer game.

The night I lost my mind
was the worst for you.
I cannot remember
all the details.
My brain has erased
most of them.
All I remember is
begging for your gun.
Promising that I was
just curious about it.
I could not understand
why you were so mad
or why you wouldn't
tell me the color of the gun.
I remember getting mad
until I started laughing.
It worked because you
finally told me it was black.
I told you to relax,
that was not the gun
I imagined using.
The one in my dreams
was silver.
You stayed until I fell asleep.

However,
nothing was ever the same.
Eventually,
it led to our demise.

Anchoring Me

It may be years
before we ever
meet again.
But somewhere
in your world,
there's a box.
It's colorful and
if you listen closely,
there's music playing
inside of it.
It used to be mine
and I've given up
on ever getting it back.
Until then,
please know
that piece of me
in your hands
can always
call me home.

"I want you, babe.
It may not be much
or what you're looking for,
but someone wants you."
You said that to me.
I refused to accept it
and you asked me
not to push you away.
I couldn't promise not to,
I was too afraid.
I didn't want to get
my hopes up and lose you.
I wish I could have
told you just how much
that statement meant and
just how much
losing you terrified me.
But I didn't.

Anchoring Me

I lived in this city
for so long,
I stopped hearing
how loud it was.
After we met,
you insisted on
pointing out every car
that beeped,
every siren,
and every crazy man cursing.
Now you're gone
and I'm stuck in a city
that never fucking sleeps.

I can't stop thinking
about the night I fell apart.
My family made me
feel like a horrible
person that night.
I wanted to give up.
But you wouldn't let me.
You fought me so hard
and promised you were
there for me.
 It was enough.
It was.
I kept pushing you away.
I insisted that everyone
would be happier
with me gone.
That I wasn't worth
all the pain I was causing.
Your reply was,
"does it look like I'm afraid
of getting my hands dirty?
You're worth it."
When did I stop being worth it?

I spent so many years
building a tower created
of bricks and steel
around me.
I wouldn't let anyone in.
I convinced myself
I was above basic human needs.
I didn't need them,
they were just a weakness.
I don't need the pain
that follows love.
Or the comfort
that comes with trust.
I was above such
trivial emotions.
Then you came along.
It took one week and I
willingly opened the door
to this tower of mine.
You showed me your heart
and I wanted to
keep it safe inside.
It happened so easily.
There was no

struggle of emotions
or a battle within.
The guards at the door
knew they should
welcome you home.
But we weren't
strong enough to
fight against the invasion
of the demons that
wanted you gone.

The high were high
and the lows, baby,
they were so fucking low.
Your hands got dirtier
than you ever expected,
didn't they?
Eventually,
you washed me off
and walked away.
But tell me,
did I at least
leave a stain?

Sometimes I wonder if
I would have ever let you go.
I like to convince myself
that we would never
have made it anyway.
That I would have
gotten bored.
Or I wouldn't have
been able to commit.
Yet, it's been months
since you left
and somehow,
I'm still completely
committed to you.
And in moments like these,
I accept the fact that
I would have been yours forever.
I was too attached
to truly let you go.

I've always believed
that soulmates would have
an earth shattering connection
when they finally meet.
That it would be full of fire.
I met several people
that have fit into that.
The flames blew strong
but were quickly
extinguished.
The pain of losing them
was so intense,
they had to be my soulmate.
I never felt that with you.
I assumed it meant you
weren't my soulmate.
I couldn't stay away though.
I loved being around you.
I loved hearing your voice.
It felt too easy.
It felt too normal,
as if this has been done
so many times before.
It wasn't hard

to open up to you.
It didn't take long
to trust you.
Losing you didn't
cause me pain,
it just made me shut down
for a while.
Maybe that's how
soulmates are.
That feeling of
picking up
where you left off.
Is that why I shut down
when I lost you?
Because my soul was
too defeated to cope?
Did we fuck this lifetime up?

It's a sad story,
the one about
the sun and the moon.
They are both light.
But the sun shines
so brightly while the moon
is confined to darkness.
They rarely meet.
When they do finally touch,
the moon kills the sun's
warm light and casts
a darkness on the world.
Is that what we are?
You the sun,
and me, the moon?
Well then,
I won't offer you the moon.
I'm too addicted to your light.

Please don't forget
how hard I fought for you.
I would have fought harder
if I was fighting
everything but you.
But I'll respect your wishes
and lay down my weapons.

The pedestal I built you
has taken up so much room.
I have cleaned as much
as I can but,
there's no space left
for anyone else.
So, I'm sorry love,
but I think I'm ready
to break down the
statue of you.

It felt both wrong
and cleansing
to let someone else
touch the spots
that once belonged
to you.

I've let several people
into my tower
after you left.
It was too quiet
to stay there alone.
They have been
polite guests and
tried to take care of me.
I appreciated their
efforts and kindness.
They made me laugh
and laid their hearts
on my floors.
I wish you could
meet them.
On some nights,
when missing you
becomes too much to bear,
I visit your room
in the deepest chambers
of this tower of mine.
I wouldn't allow
any of them
into the room

that belonged to you.
After all,
they are only guests
in your home.

I told my friend about you today.
I started at the beginning ,
which never felt new at all.
I told her how it always felt
like coming home.
I told her about the way
your voice could calm
everything inside of me.
I told her about
the instant recognition.
And I told her about
how your laugh
literally made my world
feel brighter than ever,
like there was somehow
more sun than usual.
I told her about the
magnetic pull I felt
and how it might be
older than either of us.
And she told me,
that every time I mention you,
it sounds like pure poetry.

I used to complain to you
because I was too happy.
I loved being around you
so much that I couldn't
focus on anything else.
I blamed you for
ruining my writing career.
Every writer knows
they can't produce anything
incredible if they are too happy.
You took my complaining
as a compliment.
And you should,
I've never been as happy
as I was with you.
Now you're gone
and my very first collection
will be released in
less than two weeks.

Can I throw it all away
and have you back instead?
Fuck this career.
I've always needed you more.

I have always thrown
people away easily.
Once someone leaves,
I am incapable of
letting them back in.
I do forgive,
not for them,
but for myself.
However,
my guards keep
them far away.
They are quick to
shoot them down
if they get too close.
No questions asked.
Yet, I can't understand
why those guards
still search for you
every day.
I don't understand
why they are desperate
to let you back in.
I have no idea
how you created

a soft spot within this tower.
It isn't even mine anymore.
It's yours.

Anchoring Me

I want you, love.
It may not be much
or what you're looking for,
but someone wants you.

Yeah, I'm insane.
Yeah, maybe you want
something better.
But just remember,
someone will always
be waiting for you.

I know I was difficult.
I know being with me was hard.
I have so many demons
and some days
I'm consumed with darkness.
Wasn't I worth a fight though?
I tried to make you happy.
Didn't I deserve for you
to fight for me?
Even if the person you
were fighting was me?
Were the good days
not worth it?
Was I not worth it?

Sometimes,
when I really miss you,
I think about that
month we were busy.
I had holidays and
you were traveling.
The time apart caused fights
because I was missing
you so much.
We weren't used to
not talking all day.
I'm sorry that
I ruined that trip
for you.
I was not used to
being in a love
that consumed me.

I was so mad when you got home.
I convinced myself you were
partying with your co-workers
and having a great time
because I wasn't there.
But I remember

your reply perfectly.

"Hotels are fun,
I do like seeing everyone.
But I really missed you.
I'm happy to finally be home."

Maybe you were
missing your bed.
But I really believed
that your home
was with me.

I am stubborn
and my fuse is short.
 I'm also kind and
my heart is big.
I speak without thinking
but I loved making you laugh.
I am insensitive
but I cared more
than you understood.
I am impatient
and unreliable.
I admit it,
I even litter.
But I would try to
fix this world for you.
And then,
I'd turn around
and burn it down
if you asked me to.

I bet your insecurity
is convincing you
that I'm better off.
Or that you should back off.
Maybe you believe
we won't ever make it.
Or that you aren't
good enough for me.
Fine. Be insecure.
Convince yourself
that you'll be happier
without me.
But don't ever claim
you stayed away for me.

Anchoring Me

I heard your name today,
in the same way
I used to use it
with the same
subtle note of pure affection.
I heard your name today,
from the lips of
a total stranger.
And it still tugged
on my heart to
feel you that close again

I spend most of my day
trying to unlove you.
But instead,
I give up
and hate myself
for still wanting someone
who is long gone.

I threw it all away,
every item of clothing
that you picked out,
every item that
reminds me you.
Except one.
The blue one,
remember?
I wanted to hold on
to one more thing
that was yours.
But I refuse to wear it.
I barely wear white either.
My closet has been filled
with blues, grays,
and blacks.
As if that white period
belonged to you.
But sometimes,
I still wear that
blue piece you
picked out.
And I'm angry
at it every time.

Because how could
it still fit perfectly
when you are
no longer here?

I don't know
if you still smell like
Tom Ford perfume.
And I can't remember
the way your laugh
sounds anymore.
But I always wish
 I asked you to stay.

I have never heard of
a great love story
that wasn't filled with
tears, heartbreak,
and obstacles
before finally earning
a happily ever after.
And my love,
our story could
have been great.

Anchoring Me

I trusted you with my heart
and you broke it into pieces
while promising me
that all you wanted
was my happiness.

Nicole Hartley

Sometimes,
I feel myself falling in love
with you all over again,
as passionate and intense
as it used to be,
even though you are
no longer around.
And I can't help but wonder
if maybe,
darling maybe,
in another world,
we are still so
very much in love.

After you left,
I did not feel anything.
Maybe you didn't mean
that much to me.
For five months,
I felt nothing.
Now,
my blood is
quietly simmering
as the waves crash
against the walls of
this dam inside of me.
The cracks are starting
and I fear that I will not
be able to survive
the coming storm.

As the months go by,
I'm forgetting things
I wish I could hold on to.
I don't actually know
which one of us
called my nacho pizza
a poncho.
And I really wish
I remembered.
My mind has always
tried to protect me
by taking away
painful memories.
Now it has begun
erasing you.
However,
I trust my heart.
And even with
no memories,
I will still love you.

I want another chance.
I can't promise that
we'll never fight, we will.
I can't promise my demons
will disappear,
this illness can't be cured.
I can't promise
this second chance
will last forever.
But…
I can promise
to fight those demons
harder than you
could imagine.
And I can promise
to work toward forever.
I need another chance.

Oh God babe,
I was a mess, wasn't I?
There are still days that
I can't forgive myself for it.
And days that I'm so sure
of just how much
you saved me.
Even though you probably
don't realize you did.
I can feel you
worrying about me
sometimes.
Please don't.
I'm okay now.
I'm healthy.
I'm happy.
A part of me is still
very much in love
with you.
I suppose it always will be.
But the rest has moved on.

When you move on,
if you tell her anything,
tell her about the times
I read to you.
Tell her how
you hung on my
every word,
how you sighed
when I finished.
Tell her how
your voice cracked
when you told me
how much you
loved that story.
Do you remember?
The one about the tree
that gives and gives
until there's nothing left.

If you tell her anything,
tell her how the world
ceased to exist every time
my voice was in your ear.
Tell her,

Nicole Hartley

that for a single moment,
our love conquered
everything.

I always miss you,
even before I knew
you existed.
I felt you
and I missed you.
Like an ache and
a longing for something
only my soul remembered
and my mind forgot.
When we finally met,
the aching stopped.
I missed you when
you were busy,
but I no longer ached.
Since you've been gone,
it has returned.
Same feeling as before,
except, it now has a face.

It's incredible how much
time has quickly passed.
I have changed
and built a new life.
But on some days,
my heart is still standing
in a world
where you once existed.

There are days when
my mind so clearly
paints your face
and your voice.
And on some days,
you are so faded
from my memory
and all I remember
is the fact that you
haven't been here
in a long time.
And love,
I don't know
which days I prefer.

If you ever wonder
whether I still love you,
the truth is,
I can't imagine
what it would feel like
to ever stop.

Even though
I wasn't ready for us,
it never stopped me
from loving you.
And now,
I don't love you anymore.
Not in the way I once did.
I'm no longer consumed
by you and us.
But I love you still,
just as intensely.
In the way that
my heart is still
so completely
yours.

It's been years since we ended.
I'm a new person now
and you wouldn't recognize me.
I found someone new.
Someone, who takes me
to soccer games
and fulfills all the promises
that you never did.
And I love in a way
I don't fully understand.
A safe way.
I no longer cry myself
to sleep at the thought of you.
I can breathe,
even at the mention
of your name.
Yet, a piece of me
misses you,
no longer as a lover,
but as a piece of me
that belongs close by.

Anchoring Me

I have spent a long time
trying to figure out
what we were.
You were always
an almost,
even though
you felt like a home.
Maybe you were a lover,
a best friend,
a first love.
Finally,
I asked the universe,
the stars,
and a good soul
to help me.
What were you?
Why did you consume
my heart and soul
for so much longer
than you were welcome?
And I watched,
as she anchored
the universe into her cards
to give me the answer I needed.

What were you?
The answer was
what I always knew
and what I always feared
would be true.
We were two souls
split apart from
the same fire.
It makes sense.
Even though you were
in my life for such
a short time,
even though
it was such a mess.
It was what I needed
to guide me toward
my new path
on this earth.

Acknowledgements

This journey and this book would not have been possible if it weren't for all the incredible people in my life. I survived a rough past, a mental illness, and a heartbreak that I was sure I would never recover from. Today, I am a new person, filled with so much love, passion, motivation, and happiness. That would never have been possible if it weren't for my amazing friends who are more like my family.

Kris, I'm not sure I would have gotten over this heartbreak if it weren't for you. Thank you for supporting me, for listening to me cry without ever telling me I needed to let go, for editing my work, and for giving me the clarity I desperately needed.

Saide, you have shown me that family isn't always defined by blood. I can choose my family and you have always been an easy choice. Thank you for being here for me even on the days you wanted to kill me.

Karla, you were my very first real friend. I know I always say that but it has meant so much to me. I learned how to trust and open up. Thank you for sticking by me even though I didn't make it easy. Thank you for editing this book and yelling at me until I allowed myself to be more vulnerable.

Alicia, you have not only healed me, but you have taught me how much I'm worth. You deserve so much more than I can give you. Thank you for teaching me how to love and be loved in return.

Dana, you have believed in me so much more than I ever believed in myself. I would have never gotten to where I am today if it weren't for your presence in my life. You are my biggest fan and I can't imagine loving myself if it weren't for you. Thank you for being here every day, for your kindness, and your complete faith in me.

Carlos, you have been the big brother I always wanted. You have seen me for who I am from day one. Thank you for showing me that good men exist.

There are so many people that need to be included, so many people that believed in me, supported me, and taught me what friendship really means. A few people that have made a difference in my life, Dor, Wade, Sakshi, Rosa, Kinley, Cas, Chelsie, Chloe, AJ, Amy, Hiya, Natalie, and Sarah.

We may not be in each other's lives daily, but please know that you made a difference in mine. And of course, thank you to every person that has read any of my words. You have encouraged me and saved me more than you know.

A huge thanks to Nour Tohamy and Patrick Montanaro for helping me create the incredible cover.

- Nicole Hartley

Thanks for reading! Come find me and tell me what you thought ☺

@NicoleHartley22